CHICAGO STATIONS & TRAINS PHOTO ARCHIVE

John Kelly

D1737068

Iconografix

Iconografix
PO Box 446
Hudson, Wisconsin 54016 USA

Library of Congress Control Number: 2008923170

ISBN-13: 978-1-58388-216-0
ISBN-10: 1-58388-216-2

08 09 10 11 12 13 6 5 4 3 2 1

Printed in China

Cover and book design by Dan Perry

Copyediting by Andy Lindberg

Cover photo-Erie passenger train number 6, The Lake Cities led by EMD E8 locomotive 820, departed Dearborn Station, circa 1950s. The Lee Overalls sign and Chicago skyline were often visible in photos of Dearborn Station. *JM Gruber collection*

BOOK PROPOSALS

Iconografix is a publishing company specializing in books for transportation enthusiasts. We publish in a number of different areas, including Automobiles, Auto Racing, Buses, Construction Equipment, Emergency Equipment, Farming Equipment, Railroads & Trucks. The Iconografix imprint is constantly growing and expanding into new subject areas.

Authors, editors, and knowledgeable enthusiasts in the field of transportation history are invited to contact the Editorial Department at Iconografix, Inc., PO Box 446, Hudson, WI 54016.

www.iconografixinc.com

Table of Contents

Acknowledgements

Chicago's railroad stations served as the center of rail travel across the United States for many years. After private railroad passenger service ended in 1971, Amtrak chose Chicago Union Station as their Midwest hub in 1972. Having seen so many years of service, Union Station needed remodeling and in 1991 Amtrak spent $32 million on a two-year renovation. When the restoration was complete, Union Station's original Beaux-Arts style remained intact, but with a modern-day look. The main waiting room's vaulted skylights once again beam sun onto high-back wood benches. Travelers enjoy the expanded food court and Amtrak's Metropolitan Lounge for sleeping car passengers.

Over the years I have made frequent trips on Metra's Northwest Line to North Western Station, and it has been fun to walk around that station and also Dearborn Station's former head house (now offices and shops). While waiting to board Amtrak on a number of trips out of Union Station, I have always enjoyed the ornate architecture with pink Tennessee marble floors, terracotta walls, grand staircases and large station clock. Union Station reminds me of the streamlined era with colorful trains like the Zephyr, Hiawatha and Broadway Limited. It was exploring those three stations that inspired me to write Chicago Stations and Trains.

Friends JM Gruber (Mainline Photos), Bill Raia, Douglas Wornom, Kent Ohlfs, Jay Williams and John Gruber contributed historic station photos from their collections, and I thank them. Dennis McClendon and Chicago CartoGraphics supplied maps of Chicago Stations. Thanks also to my partner, and train riding companion Linda Shult for her proofreading skills, and to the Iconografix staff for publishing this book.

Introduction

No other American city had such a fascinating group of railroad passenger stations as Chicago. This book highlights Chicago's six major railroad stations and the trains that served them. Included are Dearborn Station, Grand Central Station, Central Station, La Salle Street Station, North Western Station, and Union Station. Of these, only the last two are operating today. Three commuter stations also served Chicago: Illinois Central's Randolph Street Station (now Millennium Station), Chicago North Shore & Milwaukee Railroad's Roosevelt Road Station, and Chicago Aurora & Elgin's Wells Street Terminal.

Railroad stations were once the grand dames of large American cities. Each urban station had its own unique architecture and each served as city gateway with a maze of tracks, platforms and multicolored passenger trains. The maintenance facilities connected to most big-city railroad stations provided locomotive service for coal and water (and later, diesel fuel), mail and express loading, coach cleaners, laundry service for sleeping cars, and commissary food service for dining cars. In addition, most large stations had a great hall or waiting room that typically offered ticket counters, baggage storage room, redcap stand, information kiosk, newsstand, lunchroom, telephones, washrooms, and passenger seating. The part of the station comprising these functions was often called the "main station" or "head house." Another part of the station, called the "concourse," was generally an enclosed building connected to the head house, often built perpendicular to the tracks below. Passengers gathered in the concourse area prior to departure, where conductors collected their tickets and ushered them to the boarding gates and departure tracks. At track level, passengers were protected from the elements by platform canopies or elaborate, arched-roof train sheds.

In the early years of the 20th century many American cities like Chicago built magnificent train stations that became symbols of their cities' cultural sophistication, wealth and development.

Chicago railroad station architecture can be summarized into three distinct styles, Romanesque, Beaux-Arts and Moderne (Art Deco). In the late 1800s, the Romanesque style featured dark stonework with steeply pitched rooflines and tall clock towers. The style was patterned on medieval Italian architecture, made popular by architect Henry Hobson Richardson. The 1893 World's Columbian Exposition in Chicago had profound impact on railroad station design and public buildings in America. Many stations were modeled on the European Beaux-Arts style, featuring columns, ornamentation and cavernous interior rooms built of stone, marble or brick. Beaux-Arts style incorporated the City Beautiful movement championed by Chicago architect Daniel Burnham, whose "Make No Little Plans" credo became architectural legend. City Beautiful sought to clean up industrial America by incorporating park-like settings with formal gardens and green spaces. In 1925, the International Exhibition of Modern Decorative and Industrial Arts, held in Paris, revolutionized the design world with a style called Moderne, sometimes referred to as Art Deco. The signature elements of Moderne were curvilinear forms, sleek lines and smooth surfaces.

Dearborn Station was the oldest and smallest of the six major Chicago railroad stations, but one of the busiest, hosting six of the 20 passenger railroads that served Chicago. Originally known as Polk Street Depot, it was located at South Dearborn and West Polk Street, and served six railroads including Santa Fe, Chicago & Eastern Illinois, Erie, Grand Trunk, Monon, and Wabash. Dearborn Station was managed by the Chicago & Western Indiana Railroad, which was owned by five of the six railroads using the station, except for tenant Santa Fe. The Romanesque red-granite station with twelve-story clock tower was designed by Cyrus L. W. Eidlitz, and opened May 8, 1885. Inside the station were ticket counters, waiting room and a Fred Harvey Lunch Room. Behind the head house was the wooden train shed with truss-supported platform canopies over the tracks. Following World War II, the station was retrofitted in the Moderne style (Art Deco), with marble walls, fluorescent lighting, and sliding glass train gates. Dearborn Station closed May 2, 1971, as part of Amtrak's consolidation of intercity train operations to Chicago Union Station. The train shed was torn down in 1976 and the station was abandoned until 1980, when the Chicago urban renewal community built Dearborn Park on former approach tracks and yards south of the station. Today, Dearborn Station's head house survives as a railroad landmark with retail and office space in Chicago's Printer's Row neighborhood.

Grand Central Station was originally built for the Wisconsin Central Railroad and the Chicago and Northern Pacific Railroad; it opened December 8, 1890. The station was designed by Solon Spencer Berman, who gained notoriety as the designer of the Pullman Company neighborhood on Chicago's south side. Following Wisconsin Central financial troubles in 1910, control of Grand Central Station passed to the Baltimore & Ohio Chicago Terminal Railroad. Grand Central was located at the southwestern part of the Chicago Loop between Harrison and Wells Street, along the south branch of the Chicago River. The Romanesque brick and brownstone L-shaped station was 225-feet wide facing Harrison Street and 471-feet long facing Wells Street. Outstanding features were the 247-foot clock tower and the arched glass and steel, stub-end train shed, 119 feet wide and 555 feet long. Heavy, wrought iron gates led to the head house with beautiful stained-glass windows in the 70- by 200-foot columned waiting room. Never a busy station, Grand Central evoked the glamour of railroading's early years with its famous Baltimore & Ohio Capitol Limited passenger train. Other tenants included Chicago Great Western, Pere Marquette and Soo Line. Following Grand Central's closing on November 8, 1969, C&O and B&O trains transferred to Chicago & North Western Station. Grand Central Station was razed in 1971 and today a mixed condominium-retail complex is on the former site.

Occasionally referred to as 12th Street Station, Illinois Central's Central Station was located at the southern end of Grant Park at Roosevelt Road (12th Street) and Michigan Avenue. Suitable to the era, the Romanesque structure was designed by Bradford Gilbert and opened April 7, 1893, in time for the World's Columbian Exposition. The nine-story station housed the general offices of the Illinois Central Railroad and featured a 13-story clock tower. At one time, Central Station had the largest train shed in the world, measured at 140 by 610 feet. Although Illinois Central intercity trains originated or terminated at Central Station, the station had run-through trackage for Illinois Central electric and South Shore commuter trains leading to Randolph Street Station (now Millennium Station) one mile north. Illinois Central's Panama Limited and City of New Orleans used Central Station, as did New York Central subsidiary Michigan Central and Big Four Route. Through the years other tenant railroads included Chesapeake & Ohio, Soo Line and Penn Central. Central Station survived into the Amtrak era when the last trains departed March 5, 1972. The station was demolished in 1974 and today is the site of the fashionable Central Station Square condominiums.

La Salle Street Station was situated in the heart of the Chicago Loop at La Salle and Van Buren Street, with the elevated transit system at its front door. Opened July 1, 1903, La Salle was designed by the Chicago firm of Frost and Granger for the Lake Shore & Michigan Southern (part of New York Central System) and the Chicago, Rock Island & Pacific. The 12-story La Salle Station's head house looked like other 20th century stone and brick office buildings in Chicago's nearby financial district. The building served as headquarters for the Rock Island Railroad and the Chicago Division offices of Nickel Plate Road and New York Central. For a short time following World War II, La Salle Station was the second busiest station in Chicago. The station included two levels: passenger ticket counters, baggage and mail facilities were on the first floor; the second floor, reached by escalator, held the waiting room, concourse and tracks. La Salle's most famous train was New York Central's 20th Century Limited, followed by the Rock Island Rockets and Golden State. Rock Island continued train service until 1978 and the station was razed in 1981 for the Chicago Stock Exchange, and in its place a commuter facility was built for Metra's Rock Island District trains.

When North Western Station (C&NW) on Madison and Canal Street opened January 3, 1911, it was the largest of Chicago's passenger stations. The Beaux-Arts style building was planned by the same Chicago firm (Frost & Granger) that designed La Salle Station. Six approach tracks led to the station's 16 stub-end tracks under the 894-foot train shed. In addition to serving C&NW's extensive commuter fleet extending north, northwest and west from downtown Chicago, C&NW Station was also home terminal for the "400 Fleet" of midwestern streamliners. From the 1930s until October 1955, C&NW operated passenger trains in partnership with Union Pacific and Southern Pacific. C&NW referred to this joint venture as "Gateway to the West," with famous name trains like City of Los Angeles, City of San Francisco, City of Portland, City of Denver and Challenger, arriving and departing from North Western Station. In 1984, the station's head house was demolished and a modern glass-sheathed office tower was built, named the Northwestern Atrium Center. In 1997, it was renamed the Ogilvie Transportation Center, and today Metra commuter trains operate from the station.

Chicago Union Station was constructed during the Roaring Twenties and the Jazz Age, opening July 23, 1925. The station was designed in the ornate Beaux-Arts style by two firms, Graham, Burnham & Company from 1913 to 1917, and by Graham, Anderson, Probst & White after 1917, and built on the west side of the Chicago River between Adams and Jackson Street. Union Station comprised two buildings: the head house and concourse. The colonnade-fronted head house on the west side of Canal Street provided eight stories for offices and featured a main waiting room with a 112-foot, vaulted ceiling and skylights, plus ticket windows and Fred Harvey Lunch Room. The concourse building on the east side of Canal Street included baggage counters, information desk, and newsstand, shops and train gates. An underground passageway connected both buildings with below-street-level track layouts in the form of two back-to-back, stub-end terminals. The station's slogan was "Crossroads of the Nation" and served multiple roads including the Pennsylvania Railroad, Burlington Route, Milwaukee Road and tenant Alton Railroad (later Gulf, Mobile & Ohio). Nine stub-end tracks faced north, accommodating Milwaukee Road passenger trains including the Hiawatha fleet. The south side of the station had 13 stub-end tracks for the Pennsylvania Railroad, Burlington Route and Alton Railroad. Name passenger trains included the Broadway Limited, California Zephyr and the Burlington Zephyr fleet. In addition, Great Northern's Empire Builder and Northern Pacific's North Coast Limited reached Chicago via the Burlington Route from the Twin Cities. Two tracks adjacent to the Chicago River allowed run-through train operations when needed. It was the busiest of Chicago's six stations, with approximately 200 daily arrivals-departures, including suburban trains. In 1969, Union Station's splendid concourse building was razed for the Gateway Central office complex. In 1972, Amtrak began using the former head house as their Chicago hub. After years of service, the station had begun to show its age, and in 1991 Amtrak began a $32 million, two-year remodeling project. They chose to retain the Beaux-Arts style and today Chicago Union Station has a modern look with enlarged concourse waiting areas, improved lighting, better train-gate access, and Metropolitan Lounge for passengers traveling first-class.

Chicago's railroad stations featured superb architecture with marble floors and staircases, while restaurants, newsstands and shops filled the concourse areas. Steel latticework beams helped support glass-domed roofs and public address systems echoed train information throughout the high-ceiling stations. Huge station clocks loomed above the brass and neon train bulletin boards that listed "On Time" trains. Beyond the boarding gates, the constant parade of trains sounded with clanging bells and rumbling steel wheels. That exciting era came to an end as airlines, automobiles and interstate highways gradually changed the way Americans lived and traveled.

By the late 1960s, the great Chicago railroad stations that had resounded with the hustle of travelers and the clatter of baggage carts began to resemble relics of a fallen empire. Fortunately the late 1980s and early 1990s offered a new beginning for two Chicago railroad stations.

Thanks to cooperating efforts among Amtrak, Metra, federal grants and some private funding, Chicago Union Station—like Boston South Station, Washington Union Station, and Los Angeles Union Station—now combines Amtrak service and commuter rail with restaurants and shops. The architectural integrity of those beautiful stations has been preserved and today they are used by suburban commuters and Amtrak passengers.

Chicago Loop and Stations circa 1930, courtesy Dennis McClendon and Chicago CartoGraphics. (See the same area circa 2000, in a map at the end of the book).

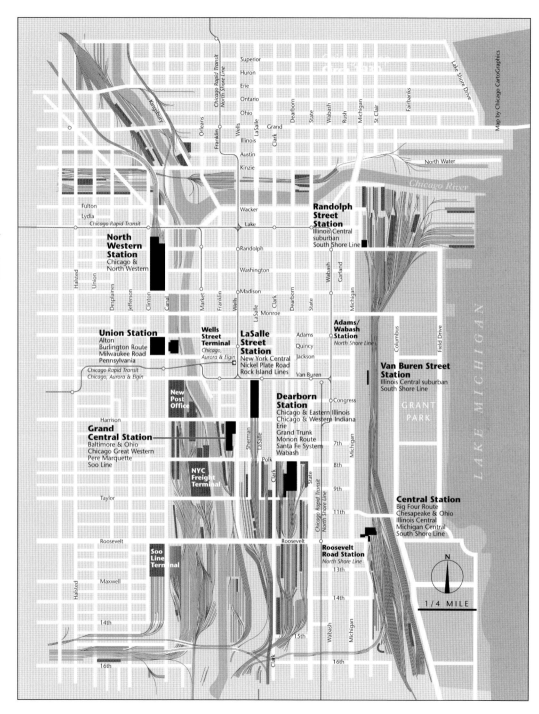

Chapter 1. Dearborn Station 1885-1971.

Chicago & Western Indiana, Chicago & Eastern Illinois, Erie, Grand Trunk, Monon Route, Santa Fe System, Wabash Railroad.

Dearborn Station was located at Polk and Dearborn Streets in downtown Chicago, seen here on July 28, 1970. Originally named Polk Street Station, it opened May 8, 1885, and was managed by the Chicago & Western Indiana Railroad. *Bill Raia collection. Postcard, author collection*

Santa Fe's first sets of diesel electric passenger locomotives were placed in service on the Super Chief, May 12, 1936. Units 1 and 1A posed at Dearborn Station in their golden olive paint scheme with the Santa Fe Indian logo on the sides. *Wendle Ranke photo, Bill Raia collection*

The first Santa Fe streamlined passenger coach was 3070, built by the Budd Company and displayed at Dearborn Station, circa 1936. *JM Gruber collection*

In May 1937, Santa Fe replaced heavyweight passenger cars on its premier trains with new lightweight, stainless steel cars and held an open house for the public at Dearborn Station. *Wendle Ranke photo, Bill Raia collection*

"The Chief is still the Chief," proclaimed this Santa Fe magazine advertisement with bold graphics. *Author collection*

On February 12, 1938, Santa Fe proudly displayed another modern set of streamlined passenger trains at a Dearborn Station open house. From the right were diesel locomotive 6 (El Capitan), steam locomotive 3460 (Chief), and diesel locomotive 3 (Super Chief). *JM Gruber collection*

The El Capitan and Chief observation cars in gleaming stainless steel posed at Dearborn Station, February 14, 1938. *JM Gruber collection*

New World Standard in Travel

Super Chief *daily between Chicago-Los Angeles*

featuring the Turquoise Room

From the flanges on the wheels
to the tip of the Pleasure Dome,
the Super Chief is new—entirely new.
The keynote is comfort.
You will find it in the distinctive
Turquoise Room...you will find it
in the Pleasure Dome...you will
find it in the dining car.
Beautiful all-room accommodations
are designed to pamper you
every mile of the way.
To give you the smoothest ride
of your life on rails, the new *Super Chief*
glides on cushioned springs...
revises any idea you have ever
had about any train.

The Santa Fe's flagship passenger train was the Super Chief, featuring the "Turquoise Room," a private dining room for 12 within the dining car. *Travel brochure, author collection*

The streamlined Super Chief-Train 17 westbound was ready to depart Dearborn Station on its transcontinental run to Los Angeles in April 1949. Fairbanks-Morse Erie-built locomotive 90 looked sharp leading the train, dressed in red, yellow and silver Warbonnet colors. It was referred to as "Train of the Stars" because of the many celebrities who traveled on the streamliner between Los Angeles and Chicago. *D. Christensen photo, Bill Raia collection*

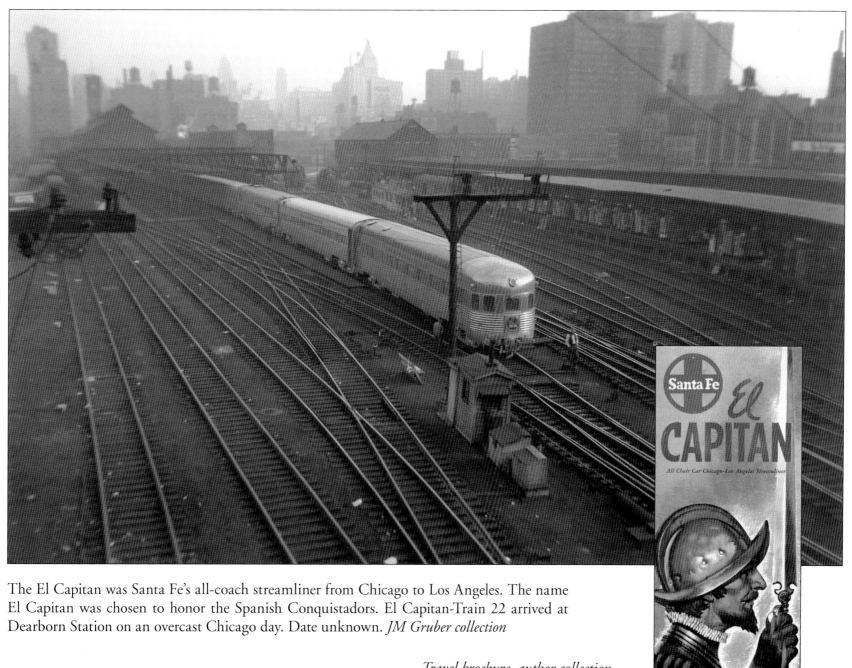

The El Capitan was Santa Fe's all-coach streamliner from Chicago to Los Angeles. The name El Capitan was chosen to honor the Spanish Conquistadors. El Capitan-Train 22 arrived at Dearborn Station on an overcast Chicago day. Date unknown. *JM Gruber collection*

Travel brochure, author collection

This north view of Dearborn Station's train shed and truss-supported platform canopies (center) includes U.S. Mail trucks and 1960s vintage automobiles, photographed from the Roosevelt Road overpass. *Doug Wornom collection*

New!
San Francisco Chief

**NEW LUXURY STREAMLINER VIA THE ROMANTIC INDIAN COUNTRY
BETWEEN CHICAGO AND SAN FRANCISCO...
WITH THROUGH SERVICE BETWEEN NEW ORLEANS-HOUSTON-SAN FRANCISCO**

Now ... to that storied city of the Golden Gate ... a brand new way to go. Santa Fe all the way. On the new *San Francisco Chief!*

Aboard this newest Santa Fe streamliner you follow the famous route of the Chiefs. Through the fabulous Indian Country in daylight—most colorful part of America!

Chair car or Pullman, you ride in smooth, swift, streamlined luxury. You ease yourself into an angled sofa seat in the new full-length Dome with its big picture windows. You have fun, make new friends in the intimate cocktail lounge below.

Every modern travel convenience is yours. Radio and recorded music throughout the train. Courier-Nurse service. Fred Harvey food. Easy connections for Yosemite National Park.

On your next trip to San Francisco, ride a great new Chief ... the *San Francisco Chief!*

San Francisco Chief running through the Indian Country of New Mexico.

The San Francisco Chief, inaugurated in June 1954, operated from Chicago to San Francisco via Amarillo, Texas, and Barstow, California, following Santa Fe's mainline through the Central Valley to Oakland. The San Francisco Chief was one of the last streamliners introduced after World War II. *Author collection*

A Red Cap porter unloaded luggage from the San Francisco Chief after its arrival at Dearborn Station. The train sported a lighted drumhead sign attached to the last car in April 1971. *Doug Wornom photo*

The Grand Canyon Limited was named for one the most popular tourist attractions along the Santa Fe Railway. Train 23 westbound and Train 24 eastbound operated on the Chicago–Los Angeles route with connections to the Grand Canyon at Williams, Arizona. In 1962, five Santa Fe F7 locomotives were leading the Grand Canyon Limited from Dearborn Station. *Jay Williams collection*

Santa Fe PA locomotive 67 had just departed Dearborn Station with a westbound passenger train. Note the Erie Railroad water tower on top of the freight house. Date unknown. *JM Gruber collection*

Santa Fe's 85-foot baggage-crew dormitory car 3477 was photographed at Dearborn Station, September 28, 1969. Note the car's connection to the Santa Fe Hi-Level coach (left). *Owen Leander photo, JM Gruber collection*

In 1951, Santa Fe introduced the "Pleasure Dome" Pullman-built, lightweight lounge-dome cars for their premier Super Chief passenger train. Santa Fe lounge-dome car 505 was photographed in Chicago. Note the "Ship and Travel Santa Fe" sign in the background. *JM Gruber collection*

Santa Fe's lounge-dome car 504 was photographed at the railroad's 21st Street Coach Yard in Chicago on April 30, 1971. *Owen Leander photo, JM Gruber collection*

Grand Trunk Western's Maple Leaf-Train 20 (Chicago–Toronto), led by steam locomotive 6320, was ready to depart Dearborn Station, August 13, 1955. Note the Lee Overalls sign on the building in the background. *Jim Scribbins photo, Bill Raia collection*

The Chicago, Indianapolis & Louisville Railway, known as the Monon, also used Dearborn Station. In 1929, steam locomotive K-1 431 switched the Hoosier (Chicago–Indianapolis) passenger train at Dearborn Station. *Jay Williams collection*

Monon's Thoroughbred-Train 5 (Chicago–Louisville) departed Dearborn Station on July 7, 1967. Note the Chicago & Western Indiana Alco RS1 number 261, which handled switching duties for all railroads at Dearborn Station except Santa Fe. *Jim Scribbins photo, Bill Raia collection*

The Erie Railroad ran passenger trains from Jersey City, New Jersey, as far west as Chicago's Dearborn Station. On July 3, 1933, the Erie Limited led by steam locomotive 4-6-2 2932 departed Dearborn Station for Jersey City. *Jay Williams collection*

Chicago & Eastern Illinois Zipper passenger train operated from Chicago to St. Louis. The Zipper was ready to depart Dearborn Station with its open-platform, heavyweight observation car, circa 1939. *Jay Williams collection*

Public timetable, author collection

The Chicago & Eastern Illinois (C&EI) was an important link to Florida and the South with its fleet of "Dixie" passenger trains. C&EI Dixie Limited ran from Chicago to Ft. Meyers, Florida, in partnership with five railroads (Louisville & Nashville, Nashville, Chattanooga & St. Louis, Central of Georgia, Atlantic Coast Line and Florida East Coast). This C&EI Dixie Limited was photographed at Dearborn Station, circa 1940. *Bill Raia collection*

Chicago & Eastern Illinois Danville Flyer-Train 3 (Chicago–Danville) departed Dearborn Station July 7, 1967, led by F9 locomotive 1102. *Jim Scribbins photo, Bill Raia collection*

The Wabash Railroad was another road that used Dearborn Station. On September 11, 1960, The Banner Blue (Chicago–St. Louis) passenger train departed with E7 locomotive 1001 and mail and express cars, followed by heavyweight passenger cars. *Jay Williams collection*

The lunch counter at Dearborn Station was still doing a brisk business in 1970 with travelers from arriving and departing trains. *Doug Wornom photo*

After the Wabash Railroad was merged into the Norfolk & Western Railroad in 1964, Norfolk & Western continued to operate commuter trains to the suburb of Orland Park, Illinois, from trackage adjacent to Dearborn Station. Norfolk & Western GP9 locomotive 513 and its commuter train waited for the conductor's "All Aboard" in April 1971. *Doug Wornom photo*

Norfolk & Western's City of Decatur passenger train (Chicago–Decatur) departed Dearborn Station with GP9 locomotive 505 in April 1971. *Doug Wornom photo*

Just one month before the start of Amtrak, Santa Fe still maintained top-notch passenger train service with uniformed conductors and train attendants dressed in shirt and tie, long coat and cap, awaiting departure in Hi-Level car 727 from Dearborn Station in April 1971. *Doug Wornom photo*

Dearborn Street Station

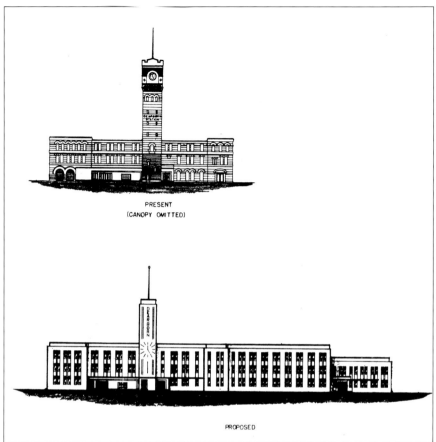

PRESENT
(CANOPY OMITTED)

PROPOSED

In 1947, there was a proposal to consolidate and modernize several of Chicago's South Loop passenger stations. These drawings were labeled Office of Terminal Engineer, June 1947. Under the consolidation, Dearborn Station would have been given Art Deco styling. *Doug Wornom collection*

Postcard, author collection

Chapter 2. Grand Central Station 1890-1969. Baltimore & Ohio, Chicago Great Western, Pere Marquette, Soo Line.

Postcard, author collection

Grand Central Station opened December 8, 1890, and was originally built by the Wisconsin Central Railroad and the Chicago and Northern Pacific Railroad. After Wisconsin Central's financial problems, control of the station passed to the Baltimore & Ohio Chicago Terminal Railroad. The station was located at Harrison and Wells Streets, and its most famous feature was the 247-foot tower clock with B&O herald. *P. Stringham photo, Bill Raia collection*

Baltimore & Ohio's premier passenger train was the Capitol Limited, with service from Chicago to Washington, D.C., and New Jersey (New York City bus connection). On August 22, 1948, Capitol Limited-Train 6, in the striking B&O blue and gray paint scheme was ready to depart Grand Central Station. *Bill Raia collection*

Another view of Baltimore & Ohio's Capitol Limited led by E8 locomotive 1446, ready to depart B&O Grand Central Station with barrel-vaulted steel train shed in the background, circa 1952. At the time of its construction, the train shed was the second largest after Grand Central in New York City. *Doug Wornom collection*

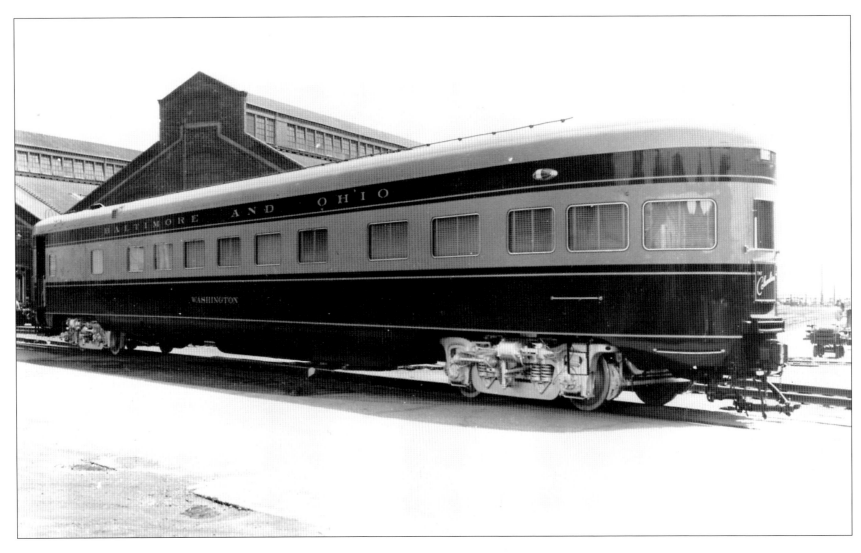

Baltimore & Ohio's observation-lounge car "Washington" was built by Pullman-Standard in 1949 for the New Columbian passenger train. Today this car is on display at the Baltimore & Ohio Railroad Museum in Baltimore. Photographed in Chicago, circa 1949. *JM Gruber collection*

Baltimore & Ohio Strata-Dome car 5551 at Chicago, April 30, 1971. Passengers enjoyed the view from the Pullman-Standard built (1949) Strata-Dome cars, complete with floodlights for nighttime viewing. Each Strata-Dome had 42 lower-level seats and 24 dome seats. *JM Gruber collection*

There's nothing like the view from
B&O's STRATA-DOME

When you travel in a B&O Strata-Dome you'll marvel at the thrilling panorama and natural beauty of the ever-changing scenery.

FLOODLIGHTS AT NIGHT

Powerful floodlight beams provide a novel view of the landscape after dark.

This exclusive B&O service between Washington and Chicago is offered at no charge!

Strata-Dome Dieseliners between
CHICAGO · AKRON · PITTSBURGH · WASHINGTON

The Capitol Limited
(All-Pullman)

The Columbian
(Deluxe Coach)

The Shenandoah *
(Pullman and Coach)

Through service to and from Baltimore, Wilmington, Philadelphia and New York.

*On the Shenandoah, Strata-Dome is operated on alternate dates. Available only to Pullman passengers on The Shenandoah.

BALTIMORE & OHIO RAILROAD
→ *Travel by train for complete relaxation* ←

This Baltimore & Ohio public timetable April 29, 1956, proclaimed, "There's nothing like the view from B&O's Strata-Dome." *Author collection*

Following Grand Central Station's closing on November 8, 1969, all C&O and B&O trains were transferred to North Western Station. This photo from April 1971, shows the Capitol Limited leaving Chicago, with the 100-story John Hancock Center visible in the background. *Doug Wornom photo*

The Chicago Great Western Railway used Grand Central Station for its passenger trains. On September 15, 1949, the Chicago-Oelwein (Iowa) local was led by gas-electric car 1009 with a Railway Post Office compartment. *Jim Scribbins photo, Bill Raia collection*

The Soo Line Railroad was another Midwest carrier to use Grand Central Station. The Laker was Soo's Chicago-Superior-Duluth passenger train, with through cars to Minneapolis. On March 28, 1948, Soo steam locomotive 4006 was backing the Laker into Grand Central Station's train shed to pick up head end cars. *D. Christensen photo, Bill Raia collection*

Soo Line GP9 2554 was in charge of the Laker, with head end cars being loaded at Grand Central Station, and landmark B&O clock tower in the background in April 1958. *L. Gerard photo, Bill Raia collection*

The Pere Marquette Railway operated in the Midwest Great Lakes region from Michigan to Chicago. The railroad's name train was Pere Marquette, with service from Chicago to Grand Rapids, Michigan. On September 15, 1949, Jim Scribbins photographed Train 8 departing Grand Central Station, led by E7 locomotive 103 with Railway Post Office cars and streamlined coaches. *Bill Raia collection*

Pere Marquette E7 locomotive 107 and mate with dark blue and yellow paint scheme were backing into Grand Central Station in 1947. *Jay Williams collection*

Public timetable, author collection

Standing like a sentry on guard duty in March 1971, the B&O station tower clock loomed over Grand Central Station's empty train shed prior to the building's being demolished. *Doug Wornom photo*

Grand Central was the target of long-term political efforts within city government to consolidate Chicago's south Loop railroad terminals. It was described by the *Chicago Tribune* as "decaying, dreary, and sadly out of date." Grand Central Station at Harrison and Wells Streets was razed in 1971. *Doug Wornom photo*

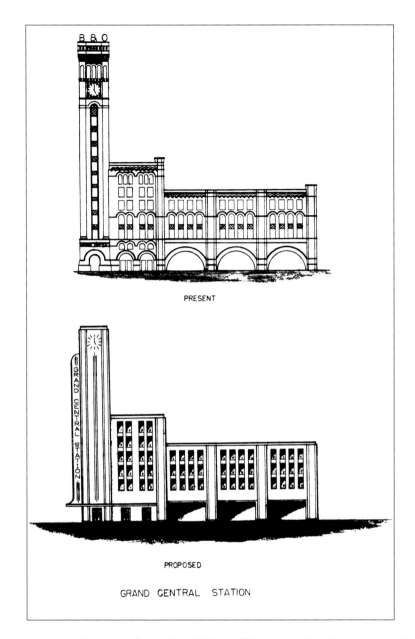

PRESENT

PROPOSED

GRAND CENTRAL STATION

Another drawing from the Office of Terminal Engineer, June 1947, shows how Grand Central Station would have looked in the streamlined redesign. *Doug Wornom collection; Postcard, author collection*

Chapter 3. Central Station 1893-1972. Illinois Central, Big Four Route, Chesapeake & Ohio, Michigan Central, South Shore Line.

Postcard, author collection

Illinois Central Railroad's Central Station was located at Roosevelt Road (12th Street) and Michigan Avenue, and often referred to as 12th Street Station. The Romanesque-style structure opened April 7, 1893, in time for the Columbian Exposition World's Fair. *April 10, 1937 photo, JM Gruber collection*

The nine-story Central Station housed the offices of the Illinois Central Railroad and featured a 13-story clock tower that could be viewed from the Chicago Loop, photographed here on April 10, 1937. *JM Gruber collection*

Illinois Central's Green Diamond streamliner was built in 1936 by Pullman-Standard and operated in Chicago-Springfield-St. Louis passenger service. The name was chosen because a green diamond was the Illinois Central logo, and the train colors were two-tone dark green with aluminum trim. The Green Diamond departed Central Station, circa 1936. *JM Gruber collection*

Public timetable, author collection

When Central Station opened it had one of the largest train sheds in the world, measured at 140 by 610 feet. In June 1936, Illinois Central steam locomotive 2434 was ready to depart the massive train shed, while the Seminole (Chicago–Jacksonville) with open-platform observation car had just arrived. *Bill Raia collection*

New York Central Railroad was a tenant of Central Station through Michigan Central and Big Four subsidiaries. The J1E Hudson locomotive 5344 was the first streamlined steam locomotive for New York Central and was leading the Mercury (Chicago–Cleveland–Detroit) from Central Station on November 11, 1939. *Wendle Ranke photo, Bill Raia collection*

Illinois Central's City of New Orleans (Chicago–New Orleans) passenger train was ready to depart Central Station in April 1971. Locomotive 4039 looked sharp in the IC orange and chocolate brown trimmed with yellow striping. Note the Illinois Central Green Diamond neon sign on the 10-story annex roof facing downtown Chicago. *Bill Raia collection*

This view of Central Station, July 5, 1956, features vintage automobiles and taxicabs, plus the art-deco style Illinois Central, Michigan Central, Big Four sign. *JM Gruber collection*

Central Station also had tracks for mail and express cars to load and unload. A New York Central boxcar is in this photo taken July 5, 1956. *JM Gruber collection*

As this photo taken July 5, 1956, shows, Central Station had nine platform tracks and was the Chicago terminal for Illinois Central passenger trains. It was also a through station for Illinois Central Electric and South Shore Electric commuter trains, ending one mile north at Randolph Street Station. *JM Gruber collection*

Illinois Central's deluxe all-Pullman streamliner, Panama Limited (Chicago–New Orleans), posed for the company photographer circa 1950s with Chicago's Michigan Avenue Skyline and Conrad Hilton Hotel in the background. *Doug Wornom collection*

Illinois Central's Governors Special (Chicago–Springfield) appears in a northward view near 18th Street, April 1971. *Doug Wornom photo*

Chapter 4. La Salle Street Station 1903-1981. New York Central, Nickel Plate Road, Rock Island Lines.

La Salle St., Station, Chicago. C. P. I. & P. R. R.-L S. & M. S. R. R.-N. Y. C. & St. L. R. R.-C. & E. I. R. R.-C. I. & S. R. R.

Postcard, author collection

The 12-story La Salle Street Station head house located at La Salle and Van Buren Streets was built to look like the other stone and brick office buildings in Chicago's nearby financial district. The building was headquarters for the Rock Island Railroad and the Chicago Division offices of New York Central and Nickel Plate Road. *Date unknown, JM Gruber collection*

This aerial view of the approach to La Salle Street Station's train shed (left) also shows B&O Grand Central Station's clock tower (right). Across the river are the Pennsylvania and CB&Q coach yards. *JM Gruber collection*

The 20th Century Limited, billed as "The Greatest Train in the World," was New York Central's all-Pullman (Chicago–New York City) flagship passenger train. For a short time following World War II, La Salle Street Station was the second busiest in Chicago for arriving and departing passenger trains. *Travel brochure, author collection*

New York Central's 20th Century Limited was ready to depart La Salle Street Station, led by a J-3A Hudson streamlined steam locomotive, with the landmark Chicago Board of Trade building in the background, circa 1938. *Bill Raia collection*

New York Central Hudson locomotive 5298 with mail and express cars waited to depart La Salle Street Station, circa 1940. *Jay Williams collection*

New York Central's Chicagoan (Chicago–New York City) rolled past the Roosevelt Road overpass on its journey to New York with mixed consist of heavyweight and streamlined cars in this July 1952 photo. *Jay Williams collection*

Rock Island's Twin Cities Express departed La Salle Street Station daily at 4:30 pm with next-day arrival in Minneapolis at 7:50 am—here on May 6, 1938. In addition to mail and express cars, the train included coaches, sleepers and diner. *Jay Williams collection*

Another view of Rock Island's Twin Cities Express leaving La Salle Street Station with 4-8-2 steam locomotive 4048, and a heavy consist of mail and express cars, circa 1950. *Jay Williams collection*

Fifteen Rock Island RS3 road switchers (485–499) were built in 1951 for Chicago suburban service. They were originally painted in Rock Island's red-black-white "wings" scheme until the 1960s, when they were repainted solid maroon. December 13, 1952. *Bill Raia collection*

Travel brochure, author collection

Rock Island's Golden State Limited (Chicago–Los Angeles) offered streamlined passenger service along the Golden State Route with partner Southern Pacific. In June 1960, the Golden State Limited, led by E8 locomotive 646, was ready to depart La Salle Street Station. *Bill Raia collection*

La Salle Street Station had seen better days when this photo was taken in January 1964. The 20th Century Limited had arrived on its overnight run from New York City, and Rock Island E8 locomotive 642 was ready to leave the station with its train. *Bill Raia collection*

Another tenant at La Salle Street Station was the Nickel Plate Road, officially known as the New York, Chicago & St. Louis Railroad. Nickel Plate's blue-and-white Alco locomotives were parked at the station next to the REA boxcar in this August 1962 photo. *Bill Raia collection*

NICKEL PLATE ROAD

Map of Business Section of Chicago

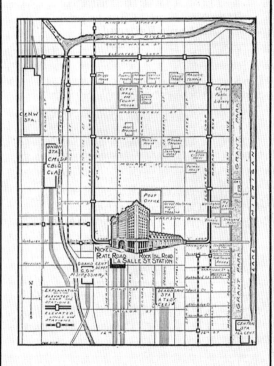

All trains of the NICKEL PLATE ROAD leave from and arrive at the La Salle St. Station, Chicago. A glance at the Map will show its convenient location and proximity to principal hotels and theatres and especially to other Railroad Stations, affording quick transfer for passengers East or West via the NICKEL PLATE ROAD.

23

NICKEL PLATE ROAD

Look for these Representatives at LaSalle St. Station, Chicago

F. J. LINDNER
Depot Passenger Agent

Mr. Lindner and Mr. Freese, the Depot Passenger Agents, have their office conveniently located near the Main Waiting Room of the La Salle Street Station. Their duties are to assist and direct passengers ticketed through, or who wish to purchase tickets via Nickel Plate Road. They will also assist passengers to their seats in Day Coaches and Sleeping Cars. Ladies traveling alone or accompanied by children, or any other person requiring unusual attention, will receive every care for their comfort and convenience.

M. F. FREESE
Depot Passenger Agent

24

This Nickel Plate Road public timetable, April 24, 1927, featured a detailed map of the Chicago Loop and photographs of the railroad's passenger agents who worked at La Salle Street Station. *Author collection*

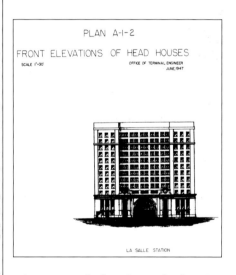

A proposed drawing of what La Salle Street Station would have looked like in a more modernized design from the Office of Terminal Engineer, June 1947. *Doug Wornom collection*

Chapter 5. North Western Station 1911 – used today by Chicago Metra.
Chicago & North Western.

The Beaux-Arts style North Western Station, located at the corner of Madison and Canal Streets in Chicago, opened January 3, 1911. In addition to Chicago & North Western (C&NW) trains, the station hosted Union Pacific "City" streamliners until October 1955. The head house was demolished in 1984 and a modern office tower built in its place. In 1997, it was renamed the Ogilvie Transportation Center and is used today by Metra commuter trains. *Bill Raia collection.*

Postcard, author collection

A Chicago & North Western public timetable, April 30, 1939, featured a full-color front cover with C&NW streamlined steam locomotives and modern diesel locomotives for Union Pacific's "City" passenger trains. *Author collection*

MAIN WAITING ROOM LOOKING TOWARD TRAIN CONCOURSE, CHICAGO AND NORTH WESTERN PASSENGER TERMINAL, CHICAGO

North Western Station featured a main waiting room with ornate marble work and bronze lamps. Six approach tracks led to the station's 16 stub-end tracks under the 894-foot train shed. *Postcards, author collection*

TRAIN SHED

STREET LEVEL LOBBY, CHICAGO & NORTHWESTERN PASSENGER TERMINAL, CHICAGO

In January 1935, C&NW premiered the 400, Chicago–Twin Cities passenger train. Leading the heavyweight 400 trains were E2-A class 4-6-2, oil-fired Pacific locomotives. Train 401 westbound for the Twin Cities was ready to leave C&NW Station in this May 26, 1938 photo. *Wendle Ranke photo, Bill Raia collection*

Travel brochure, author collection

A Chicago & North Western heavyweight, 78-foot drawing room-parlor-solarium car departed on the 400, March 27, 1938. *Bill Raia Collection*

Chicago & North Western steam locomotive 1630 was ready to depart the train shed at North Western Station with a heavyweight passenger train, July 20, 1951. *Wendle Ranke photo, Bill Raia collection*

In September 1939, C&NW upgraded the 400 to a modern streamlined train. Four new Electro-Motive E3 locomotives costing $180,000 each were ordered, along with new passenger cars painted English stagecoach-yellow and apple green. An open house at North Western Station September 18, 1939, featured the new Twin Cities 400. *Wendle Ranke photo, Bill Raia collection*

On September 19, 1939, Chicagoans lined up for tours of the Twin Cities 400 at North Western Station. *Wendle Ranke photo, Bill Raia collection*

In 1939, the streamlined Twin Cities 400, powered by EMD E3 diesel locomotives, posed at Clinton Interlocking west of the station, with Chicago's skyline in the background. *Author collection*

Union Pacific operated their "City" streamliner fleet in partnership with C&NW and Southern Pacific until October 1955. Union Pacific's City of Denver was ready to depart North Western Station (Track 5) on its first trip to Denver, June 18, 1936. Locomotive M-10005 featured automobile styling with front grille, the influence of builder Electro-Motive, a General Motors subsidiary. *Wendle Ranke photo, Bill Raia collection*

In late 1937, Union Pacific, C&NW and Southern Pacific took delivery of new trainsets for the City of Los Angeles and City of San Francisco. On January 5, 1938, the new streamliners were on display at North Western Station. From the left: City of Denver, City of Los Angeles and City of San Francisco. Note the logos of the three partner railroads on the City of San Francisco locomotive (right). *Wendle Ranke photo, Bill Raia collection*

On May 4, 1938, C&NW steam locomotive 2222 departed North Western Station with a heavyweight commuter train. *Jay Williams collection*

Chicago & North Western offered fast, frequent service to Chicagoland commuters on three routes from the west, north, and northwest into North Western Station. In 1955–1956, the C&NW commuter fleet was upgraded to modern bi-level cars from Pullman-Standard. *Doug Wornom collection*

C&NW rush hour trains at Clinton Interlocking, west of C&NW Station in this December 12, 1958, photo. *JM Gruber collection*

Chicago & North Western GP7 locomotive 1717 led a mixed commuter train of bi-level and heavyweight cars at Glen Ellyn, Illinois, circa 1956. *Author collection*

Chapter 6. Chicago Union Station 1925 – used today by Amtrak and Chicago Metra.

Pennsylvania Railroad, Burlington Route, Alton Railroad, Milwaukee Road

Chicago Union Station opened July 23, 1925, as home to four railroads, including the Pennsylvania, Burlington, Alton and Milwaukee Road. Union Station was designed as two buildings: the colonnade-fronted head house facing the west side of Canal Street, and the concourse building facing the Chicago River. *Photo and postcard, author collection*

The New Chicago Union Station is one of the "show places" of the City, and should be seen by every person visiting in or passing through Chicago.

The New Chicago Union Station

Is conceived on a most magnificent scale, equalling in general scope, as well as in detail, the finest examples of modern railway stations in the world.

Its general arrangement consists of a main building with a prolongation or concourse placed between the ends of two sets of tracks, one from the north and one from the south. The tracks and the concourse are east of Canal Street, and the main building lies between Canal, Clinton and Adams Streets and Jackson Boulevard.

The drop in the grade of the streets from the river toward the west has proved a fortunate circumstance, and has been profited by in planning the station with the waiting room on the same level as the tracks. It is a one-level station in the full meaning of the word; that is, one in which passengers find all the facilities of the station on one floor, and that the track level floor.

In a large modern terminal, as adapted to present day requirements in our metropolitan cities, it should be possible for the passenger approaching the station from any given direction to pass immediately by the most convenient route to the waiting train. Entrances and exits should, so to speak, be universal at all points of the building, so that each class of passenger traffic may take its most convenient short cut, thus minimizing confusion, loss of time, and waste of effort. This modern need of, as it were, melting the people away in the neighborhood of the station, has been made a special feature of the new terminal.

In addition to the several entrances to the main building, a convenience to passengers arriving from the loop will be the entrance to the east end of the concourse from the esplanade between the concourse and the river.

In addition to the usual conveniences of a great modern railway station, the concourse building is surrounded with ample plazas built upon railroad property with inclined ramps, stairways, special ticket office, parcel rooms, and other conveniences.

The belated passenger, whether a commuter or a long distance traveler, can enter from the point at which he first reaches the station and pass directly to his train.

One of the most important features in this same connection is the group of two automobile stands placed under cover on the track level and contiguous to the main concourse and waiting room.

The principal feature of the main building consists of a waiting room one hundred feet wide, two hundred and thirty feet long, and one hundred and ten feet high, brilliantly lighted by means of skylights in the great arched ceiling. In addition to the usual ticket and baggage facilities, this waiting room has grouped about it the restaurants, information bureau, telephone booths, telegraph office, drug store, newsstands, flower shop.

The Milwaukee Road's brochure for the opening of Chicago Union Station proclaimed it one of the "show places" of the city that "should be seen by every person visiting in or passing through Chicago." *Author collection*

Prior to Chicago Union Station's opening, railroad officials toured the concourse building still under construction. The Station Master's office was to the left and the portal under the stairs led to the Adams Street and Jackson Boulevard suburban entrances, seen here on May 22, 1925. *JM Gruber collection*

Chicago Union Station's head house featured a main waiting room with high-back wood benches for travelers. The building was still under construction as workers installed the clock in the center kiosk, May 22, 1925. *JM Gruber collection*

Postcard, author collection

Note the Beaux-Arts styling of Chicago Union Station's main waiting room with Corinthian columns, terracotta walls, pink Tennessee marble floors and a spectacular 110-foot barrel-vaulted ceiling with skylights. The Fred Harvey Lunch Room and Dining Room were to the right of this May 22, 1925, photo. *JM Gruber collection*

The Information Desk in the concourse building of Chicago Union Station helped passengers with travel and train connections. The bulletin board above the desk listed arriving train names and numbers. Three railroads (Pennsylvania, Burlington and Alton) were displayed on the board's south face, with Milwaukee Road train information on the board's north face on June 28, 1934. *JM Gruber collection*

The Chicago Transit Authority's Garfield Park Line from Chicago's west side to downtown Chicago passed the south side of Chicago Union Station's head house and concourse buildings, July 17, 1957. *JM Gruber collection*

This photo and the next look similar, but they are different. Both show the west side of Chicago Union Station's concourse building facing Canal Street. This photo has two-way automobile traffic on Canal Street. Note the 1940s vintage autos and the top of Union Station's south train sheds (right). *JM Gruber collection*

Another view of Chicago Union Station's concourse building shows traffic flow changed to northbound one-way on Canal Street, circa 1950. *JM Gruber collection*

Pennsylvania Railroad's finest passenger train was the all-Pullman, Broadway Limited (Chicago–New York City). *March 1949, travel brochure, author collection*

Pennsylvania Railroad's sleeper-lounge-observation car "Mountain View" shown at Chicago Union Station, 1961, was built by Pullman-Standard in 1949 for the Broadway Limited. *Jay Williams collection*

Pennsylvania Railroad's Admiral (Chicago–Washington–New York City) led by K4 steam locomotive 3760, crossed the south branch of the Chicago River and followed the Pennsylvania east-west main line via Ft. Wayne, Cleveland, and Pittsburgh, here on May 1, 1942. *Jay Williams collection*

Pennsylvania Railroad's coach yards on the east side of the south approach tracks to Chicago Union Station between Taylor and Lumber Streets included a mix of coach and Pullman cars, circa 1960. *JM Gruber collection*

Harrison Street Tower, located at the south end of Chicago Union Station, was where the Train Director and Levermen lined the switches and tracks for inbound and outbound trains to the station, seen here on June 20, 1975. *JM Gruber collection*

Passengers on Burlington's Morning Zephyr-Train 21 to the Twin Cities prepared to board at Chicago Union Station's concourse building, October 11, 1964. The train departed Chicago at 8 am with St. Paul arrival at 2:25 pm and Minneapolis at 2:50 pm. *John Gruber photo*

The Nebraska Zephyr (Chicago–Omaha–Lincoln), led by F7A locomotive 9924, and a California Zephyr observation car on adjoining track, appear in this April 1971 photo inside Chicago Union Station's south train shed. *Doug Wornom*

The California Zephyr "Silver Solarium" car 377 had several bedrooms and buffet-lounge-observation seating. The car was owned by the Burlington and photographed at Chicago Union Station, circa 1962. *Jay Williams collection*

Burlington's California Zephyr hustled out of Union Station for Denver, Salt Lake City and Oakland in 1962, photographed from the Roosevelt Road overpass. *Jay Williams collection*

The Afternoon Twin Zephyr departed Union Station for the trip along Burlington's Mississippi River Scenic Line, "Where Nature Smiles 300 Miles." Note three Vista-Dome cars on the short train in April 1971. *Doug Wornom photo.*

The combined Northern Pacific North Coast Limited, and Great Northern Empire Builder out of Union Station to the Twin Cities, crossed over to the center track for direct routing to Burlington's triple-track mainline, shown here April 1971. *Doug Wornom photo*

Burlington's 14th Street coach yard (right) was across from the Pennsylvania Railroad's coach yard, separated by the south approach tracks to Union Station. This view is outbound from Union Station in 1962. *Jay Williams collection*

An inbound Burlington commuter train led by E8 locomotive 9944B passed the Pennsylvania coach yard on its way to Union Station on May 21, 1950. *D. Christensen photo, Bill Raia collection*

Gulf, Mobile, & Ohio's Abraham Lincoln operated roundtrip from Chicago to St. Louis. Observation-parlor car 5998 was inbound to Union Station in this July 10, 1965, photo. *JM Gruber collection*

Milwaukee Road's Morning Hiawatha (Chicago–Twin Cities), led by stream-styled Atlantic 2, is shown on joint Milwaukee-Pennsylvania tracks near Wolf Point, where the north and south branches of the Chicago River split. Note the man in the straw hat protecting the grade crossing, circa 1936. *Jay Williams collection*

Milwaukee Road's Hiawatha, led by Atlantic 1, departed Union Station with Chicago's skyline in the background, March 27, 1938. *Bill Raia collection*

January 20, 1936, was a cold winter day in Chicago when the Hiawatha, led by Atlantic 2 with a nice head of steam, passed Milwaukee Road's Western Avenue coach yard. *Bill Raia collection*

The F-7 Hudson steam-styled locomotives arrived in 1938 to pull the longer Hiawatha trains. This photo shows F-7 102 leading a mail and express train near Chicago Union Station June 13, 1948. *D. Christiansen photo, Bill Raia collection*

This view is from Lake Street as Milwaukee Road E9 locomotive 32 C led its train into Chicago Union Station. The raised bridge in the background was on the C&NW line to Navy Pier as it crossed the north branch of the Chicago River in April 1971. *Doug Wornom photo*

Milwaukee Road's westbound Afternoon Hiawatha with glass-top Super Dome car was just minutes out of Chicago Union Station on its trip to the Twin Cities in this April 1971 photo. *Doug Wornom*

Coach passengers from the combined Union Pacific City of Denver and City of Portland walked to their coaches on the north side of Chicago Union Station, with North Western Station in the background, seen here on June 6, 1964. *John Gruber photo*

A Santa Fe Railway Fairbanks-Morse switch engine backed the Amtrak passenger train into the south train shed at Chicago Union Station June 1971. *Doug Wornom photo*

A December 1956 photo in Chicago Union Station's main waiting room captured the Milwaukee Road Choral Club singing Christmas carols, complete with Christmas tree and sunlight pouring through the windows. *Doug Wornom collection*

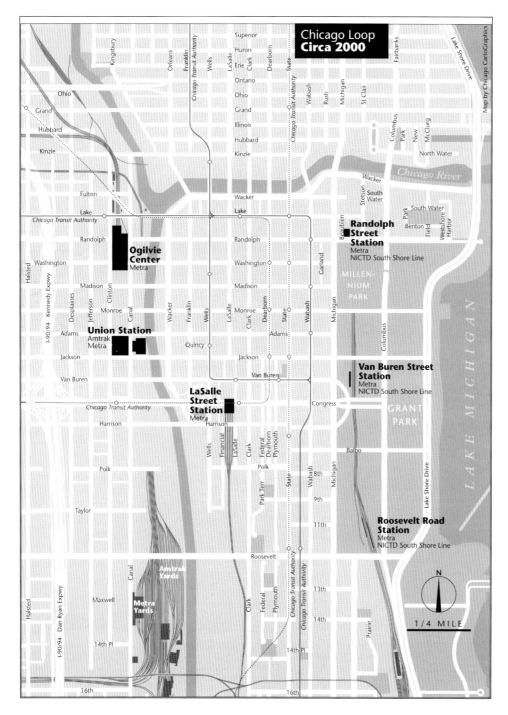

Chicago Loop and Stations circa 2000. *Courtesy Dennis McClendon and Chicago CartoGraphics*

RAILWAYS

Chicago & North Western Passenger Trains of the 400 Fleet Photo Archive ISBN 1-58388-159-X
Chicago Stations & Trains Photo Archive ISBN 1-58388-216-2
Chicago, St. Paul, Minneapolis & Omaha Railway 1880-1940 Photo Archive ISBN 1-882256-67-0
Chicagoland Commuter Railroads: Metra & Northern Indiana Commuter Transportation District ISBN 1-58388-190-5
Classic Streamliners Photo Archive: The Trains and the Designers ISBN 1-58388-144-x
Freight Trains of the Upper Mississippi River Photo Archive ISBN 1-58388-136-0
Great Lakes Ore Docks and Ore Cars ISBN 1-58388-202-2
Great Northern Railway Ore Docks of Lake Superior Photo Archive ISBN 1-58388-073-9
Illinois Central Railroad 1854-1960 Photo Archive ISBN 1-58388-063-1
Interurban Trains to Chicago Photo Archive ISBN 1-58388-199-9
Locomotives of the Upper Midwest Photo Archive: Diesel Power in the 1960s and 1970s ISBN 1-58388-113-1
Milwaukee Road 1850-1960 Photo Archive ISBN 1-882256-61-1
Milwaukee Road Depots 1856-1954 Photo Archive ISBN 1-58388-040-2
Northern Pacific Railway Photo Archive ISBN 1-58388-186-7
Pennsylvania Railroad Locomotives: Steam, Diesel & Electric Photo Archive ISBN 1-58388-228-6
Show Trains of the 20th Century ISBN 1-58388-030-5
Soo Line 1975-1992 Photo Archive ISBN 1-882256-68-9
Steam Locomotives of the B&O Railroad Photo Archive ISBN 1-58388-095-X
Trains of the Circus 1872-1956 ISBN 1-58388-024-0
Trains of the Upper Midwest Photo Archive Steam & Diesel in the 1950s & 1960s ISBN 1-58388-036-4

BUSES

Buses of ACF Photo Archive Including ACF-Brill And CCF-Brill ISBN 1-58388-101-8
Buses of Motor Coach Industries 1932-2000 Photo Archive ISBN 1-58388-039-9
City Transit Buses of the 20th Century Photo Gallery ISBN 1-58388-146-8
Fageol & Twin Coach Buses 1922-1956 Photo Archive ISBN 1-58388-075-5
Flxible Intercity Buses 1924-1970 Photo Archive ISBN 1-58388-108-5
Flxible Transit Buses 1953-1995 Photo Archive ISBN 1-58388-053-4
GM Intercity Coaches 1944-1980 Photo Archive ISBN 1-58388-099-2
Greyhound in Postcards: Buses, Depots and Posthouses ISBN 1-58388-130-1
Highway Buses of the 20th Century Photo Gallery ISBN 1-58388-121-2
*Mack® Buses 1900-1960 Photo Archive** ISBN 1-58388-020-8
New York City Transit Buses 1945-1975 Photo Archive ISBN 1-58388-149-2
Prevost Buses 1924-2002 Photo Archive ISBN 1-58388-083-6
Rapid Transit Series Buses: General Motors and Beyond ISBN 1-58388-209-X
Trailways Buses 1936-2001 Photo Archive ISBN 1-58388-029-1
Trolley Buses 1913-2001 Photo Archive ISBN 1-58388-057-7
Trolley Buses Around the World: A Photo Gallery ISBN 1-58388-175-1
Welcome Aboard the GM New Look Bus: An Enthusiast's Reference ISBN 1-58388-167-5
Yellow Coach Buses 1923-1943 Photo Archive ISBN 1-58388-054-2

EMERGENCY VEHICLES

100 Years of American LaFrance: An Illustrated History ISBN 1-58388-139-5
American Fire Apparatus Co. 1922-1993 Photo Archive ISBN 1-58388-131-X
American LaFrance 400 Series Photo Archive ISBN 1-58388-185-9
American LaFrance 500/600 Series: Photo Archive ISBN 1-58388-210-3
American LaFrance 700 Series 1945-1952 Photo Archive ISBN 1-882256-90-5
American LaFrance 700 Series 1945-1952 Photo Archive Volume 2 ISBN 1-58388-025-9
American LaFrance 700 & 800 Series 1953-1958 Photo Archive ISBN 1-882256-91-3
American LaFrance 900 Series 1958-1964 Photo Archive ISBN 1-58388-002-X
Classic Seagrave 1935-1951 Photo Archive ISBN 1-58388-034-8
Crown Firecoach 1951-1985 Photo Archive ISBN 1-58388-047-X
Elevating Platforms: A Fire Apparatus Photo Gallery ISBN 1-58388-164-6
Encyclopedia of Canadian Fire Apparatus ISBN 1-58388-119-0
Fire Chief Cars 1900-1997 Photo Album ISBN 1-882256-87-5
Firefighting Tanker Trucks and Tenders: A Fire Apparatus Photo Gallery ISBN 1-58388-138-7
FWD Fire Trucks 1914-1963 Photo Archive ISBN 1-58388-156-5
Grumman Fire Apparatus 1976-1992 Photo Archive ISBN 1-58388-165-4
Hahn Fire Apparatus 1923-1990 Photo Archive ISBN 1-58388-077-1
Heavy Rescue Trucks 1931-2000 Photo Gallery ISBN 1-58388-045-3
Imperial Fire Apparatus 1969-1976 Photo Archive ISBN 1-58388-091-7
Industrial and Private Fire Apparatus 1925-2001 Photo Archive ISBN 1-58388-049-6
*Mack Fire Trucks 1911-2005 Illustrated History** ISBN 1-58388-157-3

More Great Titles From Iconografix

All Iconografix books are available from direct mail specialty book dealers and bookstores worldwide, or can be ordered from the publisher. For book trade and distribution information or to add your name to our mailing list and receive a **FREE CATALOG** contact:

Iconografix, Inc.
PO Box 446, Dept BK
Hudson, WI, 54016

Telephone: (715) 381-9755,
(800) 289-3504 (USA),
Fax: (715) 381-9756
info@iconografixinc.com
www.iconografixinc.com

Maxim Fire Apparatus 1914-1989 Photo Archive ISBN 1-58388-050-X
Maxim Fire Apparatus Photo History ISBN 1-58388-111-5
Navy & Marine Corps Fire Apparatus 1836 -2000 Photo Gallery ISBN 1-58388-031-3
Pierre Thibault Ltd. Fire Apparatus 1918-1990 Photo Archive ISBN 1-58388-074-7
Pierce Fire Apparatus 1939-2006 Illustrated History ISBN 1-58388-189-1
Pirsch Fire Apparatus 1890-1991 Photo Archive ISBN 1-58388-082-8
Police Cars: Restoring, Collecting & Showing America's Finest Sedans ISBN 1-58388-046-1
Saulsbury Fire Rescue Apparatus 1956-2003 Photo Archive ISBN 1-58388-106-9
Seagrave 70th Anniversary Series Photo Archive ISBN 1-58388-001-1
Seagrave Fire Apparatus 1959-2004 Photo Archive ISBN 1-58388-132-8
TASC Fire Apparatus 1946-1985 Photo Archive ISBN 1-58388-065-8
The Illustrated Encyclopedia of American Fire Engine Manufacturers ISBN 1-58388-203-0
Van Pelt Fire Apparatus 1925-1987 Photo Archive ISBN 1-58388-143-3
Volunteer & Rural Fire Apparatus Photo Gallery ISBN 1-58388-005-4
W.S. Darley & Co. Fire Apparatus 1908-2000 Photo Archive ISBN 1-58388-061-5
Wildland Fire Apparatus 1940-2001 Photo Gallery ISBN 1-58388-056-9
Young Fire Equipment 1932-1991 Photo Archive ISBN 1-58388-015-1

AUTOMOTIVE

AMC Cars 1954-1987: An Illustrated History ISBN 1-58388-112-3
AMC Performance Cars 1951-1983 Photo Archive ISBN 1-58388-127-1
AMX Photo Archive: From Concept to Reality ISBN 1-58388-062-3
The American Taxi- A Century of Service ISBN 1-58388-176-X
Avanti: The Complete Story ISBN 1-58388-213-8
Buick 1946-1960 Photo Archive ISBN 1-58388-178-6
Cadillac: The Tailfin Years ISBN 1-58388-212-X
Camaro 1967-2000 Photo Archive ISBN 1-58388-032-1
Checker Cab Co. Photo History ISBN 1-58388-100-X
Chevrolet Corvair Photo History ISBN 1-58388-118-2
Chevrolet Station Wagons 1946-1966 Photo Archive ISBN 1-58388-069-0
Classic American Limousines 1955-2000 Photo Archive ISBN 1-58388-041-0
Cobra and Shelby Mustang Photo Archive 1962-2007 Including Prototypes and Clones ISBN 1-58388-198-0
The Complete U.S. Automotive Sales Literature Checklist 1946-2000 ISBN 1-58388-155-7
Corvair by Chevrolet Experimental & Production Cars 1957-1969, Ludvigsen Library Series ISBN 1-58388-058-5
Corvette The Exotic Experimental Cars, Ludvigsen Library Series ISBN 1-58388-017-8
Corvette Prototypes & Show Cars Photo Album ISBN 1-882256-77-8
DeTomaso Pantera ISBN 1-58388-177-8
Duesenberg Racecars and Passenger Cars Photo Archive ISBN 1-58388-145-X
Encyclopedia of Small-Scale Diecast Motor Vehicle Manufacturers ISBN 1-58388-174-3
Ferrari- The Factory Maranello's Secrets 1950-1975, Ludvigsen Library Series ISBN 1-58388-085-2
Ford Postwar Flatheads 1946-1953 Photo Archive ISBN 1-58388-080-1
Ford Station Wagons 1929-1991 Photo History ISBN 1-58388-103-4
Grand Prix: Pontiac's Luxury Performance Car ISBN 1-58388-184-0
Hudson Automobiles 1934-1957 Photo Archive ISBN 1-58388-110-7
Imperial 1964-1968 Photo Archive ISBN 1-882256-23-9
It's Delightful! It's Delovely! It's DeSoto Automobiles ISBN 1-58388-172-7
Jaguar XK120, XK140, XK150 Sports Cars Ludvigsen Library Series ISBN 1-58388-150-6
Javelin Photo Archive: From Concept to Reality ISBN 1-58388-071-2
The Lincoln Continental Story: From Zephyr to Mark II ISBN 1-58388-154-9
Lincoln Motor Cars 1920-1942 Photo Archive ISBN 1-882256-57-3
Mercedes-Benz 300SL: Gullwings and Roadsters 1954-1964 Ludvigsen Library Series ISBN 1-58388-137-9
Mercury Automobiles 1939-1959 ISBN 1-58388-205-7
MG Saloons and Coupes 1925-1980 ISBN 1-58388-144-1
Nash 1936-1957 Photo Archive ISBN 1-58388-086-0
Oldsmobile 1946-1960 Photo Archive ISBN 1-58388-168-9
Packard Motor Cars 1946-1958 Photo Archive ISBN 1-882256-45-X
Pontiac Dream Cars, Show Cars & Prototypes 1928-1998 Photo Album ISBN 1-882256-93-X
Pontiac's Greatest Decade 1959-1969—The Wide Track Era: An Illustrated History ISBN 1-58388-163-8
Rambler 1950-1969 Photo Archive ISBN 1-58388-078-X
Stretch Limousines 1928-2001 Photo Archive ISBN 1-58388-070-4
Studebaker Lark 1959-1966 Photo Archive ISBN 1-58388-107-7
The Collector's Guide to GTO 1964-1974 ISBN 1-58388-196-4
Thirty Years of the Volkswagen Golf & Rabbit ISBN 1-58388-158-1
Ultimate Corvette Trivia Challenge ISBN 1-58388-035-6

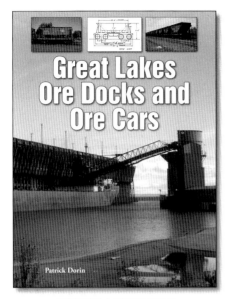

ISBN 978-1-58388-202-3

More great books from
Iconografix

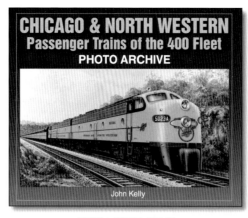

ISBN 1-58388-159-X

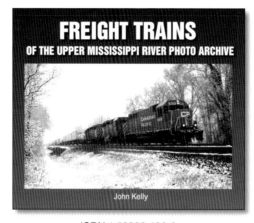

ISBN 1-58388-136-0

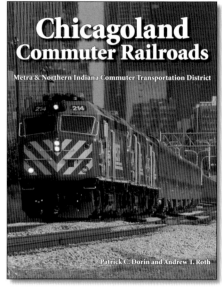

ISBN 978-1-58388-190-3

Iconografix, Inc.
P.O. Box 446, Dept BK,
Hudson, WI 54016
For a free catalog call: 1-800-289-3504
info@iconografixinc.com
www.iconografixinc.com

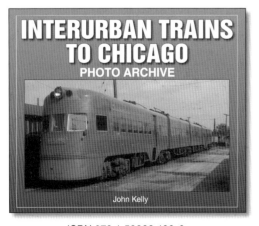

ISBN 978-1-58388-199-6

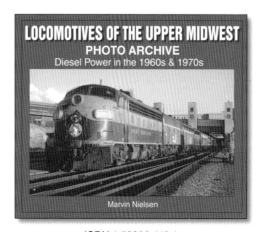

ISBN 1-58388-113-1

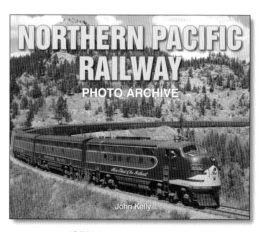

ISBN 978-1-58388-186-6